Aaron's First Poetry Book

A.W.J. Pilgrim

Text and image copyright © 2017

A.W.J. Pilgrim

This is a poetry book written by the author Aaron William James Pilgrim.

The author A.W.J. Pilgrim would like to dedicate this book to all his poetry teachers at Cooltan Arts.

Table of Contents

Introduction

-

As well as a poet, Aaron W.J. Pilgrim is also an artist painter, author, cartoonist, photographer, musici & sculptor. He grew up & lives in South East London. He lives with his partner Michelle & his daughter Grace. Aaron currently attends Cooltan Arts, that is a arts based charity for people that have suffered mental distress at some time in their life. At Cooltan Arts Aaron has been part of the poetry group for two and a half years. It is in this group, that Aaron has written all of the poetry that is in this book. Aaron has had six great poetry teachers at Cooltan Arts that are Ed Mayhew, Olivia Furber, Isley Lynne, Chase Lynne, Andrea Spitso and Karis Halsall. Most of the poetry in this book, has been written as part of a glass lesson exercise. The particular exercise is hinted at in the title of each poem. Aaron's poetry usually rhymes & is normally written in an easy to understand way. People have commented that not all the poems rhyme, but I'll let you know that they don't have to. Aaron has read his poetry at many Cootan Arts events. Including reading his poetry with the backing classical music of The Waterloo Sinfonia, at St. Johns Church, that is in Waterloo, London, which was filmed & put on YouTube. Also, at Shakespeare's 'The Globe Theatre' as part of, "The Concert for Winter, Stories of Southwark.'

Aaron really hopes that you enjoy reading his poetry as much as he enjoyed writing it, & says "happy reading."

Aaron's First Poetry Book

-

-

<u>Pictures memory technique poem</u>

Why was the finger in my car?

Then there was a cat, drinking from a goblet, how bazaar.

I see a pen dangling from a string,

& a moon as if in a dream.

Why is there a ceramic cow on the key rack?

On my bicycle, I'll make a trek,

to the settee with some baby boots.

With bricks by the garden doors, all in a group.

-

-

<u>Metaphor's for major life events.</u>

Incarceration is not always preventative.

Birth is a bird singing.

Death is a journey away.

Grief Poem

What is grief like?

This is what I feel.

A black sky never ending.

A shrieking scream of pain.

A smell of burnt rubber.

An off taste of dull sour.

With a feeling of rusted barbed wire.

Crouching, wheezing & holding its left breast.

Flooding makes UK sceptics hot under the collar

Thirty years ago, they warned us of global warming.

Thirty years on, it's happening.

But people still seem shocked & surprised,

when Summerset floods, & the water rise.

We need to do what they told us to do thirty years ago,

but to take the advice, we are still very slow.

It all comes down to money, burning fossil fuel for a greenie is not funny.

However, we are slowly changing,

& the scientist's message is now raging.

Queen Bohemian Rhapsody poem

-

Mama mia, mama mia, I'm engrossed in my poetry.

Look at me writing, & you can see.

I really matters to me, to me, to me.

Poetry, poetry, I'm out of my tree,

because I'm other worldly, writing my poetry.

-

-

The Harrods lion

-

There was a small lion cub named Christian, he was sold at Harrods.

But of course he grew, he grew, & grew some more.

So they introduced him to the wild,

this was the best thing they could do.

The owners were warned not to approach him.

They were told he's wild, & a head of a pride.

But they couldn't resist, & to the wild they went.

Along came the lion, but was still loving, like a big teddy bear.

Even the lion's new wife was friendly.

I saw this story on youtube, it's a heartwarming film,

if you watch it you'll see.

The Japanese Miami Beach

-

Sleeping rough on the beach in Japan.

Waking to the waves singing.

Where fishermen once blew on shell trumpets,

to tell their families the catch they were bringing.

A picturesque postcard in the brain.

Away from the cares of the world.

-

The pigeon story poem

-

There was a bird who was miserable.

She was a London pigeon, she was inconsolable.

She landed on a window ledge,

& listened to the humans, they had no money left.

One said, "we can't fly on holiday, no flying fun for us."

The pigeon thought, 'I suppose I'm lucky that I can fly.'

'These humans can't, no matter how hard they try.'

This fact cheered the pigeon up, & she beat her wings ready for take-off.

Freedom of the skies her wings bring.

She was now so happy, that she could sing.

The poets & bards to sing

-

Ahh poetry & bards, a whole fantastic world.

Become passionate, open a door in literature,

you'll never be poor, you'll always want more.

& singing is music to your heart.

Read one Shakespeare play, it will be a start of a wonderful thing.

You will have a cure to boredom.

& what better thing than that.

Think hard, fast & deep about your beliefs

-

I sometimes find it strange, how intelligent people believe in religion.

Did the dinosaurs never exist?

Is science nearly always wrong?

There are so many religions, is only one right?

But on the other hand, it's strange to be an atheist.

If you find a watch, someone created it.

So we have life, so who created that?

A good topic to think about,

you can often change your views.

Perhaps it's good to alter them, within reason.

This hippy music

A response to Richard Ashcroft's song, "Music is Power."

—

—

This music gets into your soul.

From your ears your visions grow.

The power of the words & melody.

Listen & you'll see.

Flower power is where it's at.

Listen to comprehend the universe.

Its megalatronic majesty, & all that.

This music is really heavy,

& it moves my soul, definitely.

A Tintorretto painting

—

Today I looked at a Tintorretto,

a painting of God in his red robe.

He was making all the animals,

in a magical way without any tools.

If you believe the world was created in seven days,

then you're a creationist I'd say.

& you'll probably like evangelists,

to be like them you probably wish.

Boom boom boom (a group exercise poem)

-

Laughing hyenas to say, 'yes.'

Ten ten ten ten, someone's dropped some pans.

He's annoyed he goes, 'arrrh.'

Arrrh the absolute pain & dread.

Better out than in.

The man doesn't find it funny.

City of the future

-

A city of the future, what is it like?

It has lots of skyscrapers, behold the sight.

Flying cars & buses, & multi-coloured parks.

Big floating billboards, shining in the dark.

So many gadgets & fuel is free.

Just use your imagination, & the future you'll see.

Freewriting in Andrea's class

—

I love my poetry lessons.

Every lesson is different from the one before.

Sometimes we have a new teacher,

with new ideas of how to write poetry.

Its good fun, the group are my friends.

We know each other well, & that is swell so say I,

So say I,

So say I.

So Thursdays are a good day.

Creativity flows from my pen,

on to some paper, given to me by Sasha.

Well I think this poem is finished, I think it's quite good.

Well this definitely is a positive piece of work.

Glad I tried once again some freewriting.

It's a type of poetry that's exciting.

Freewriting to Andrea's words

–

Aren't ballpoint pens wonderful?

You don't need a bottle of ink,

that could be knocked over by a puppy,

That could spill all over the table.

I attach a ball point pen to my calendar,

by some red string.

December has a photo of a mountain top,

with a yellow tail bird in the air.

I drew a cartoon on one of the days,

to remind me to water the plant life.

On the July page there's a photo of a lion,

with a lady in a safari jeep.

Yes I love ballpoint pens & my calendar too.

I wish for peace

-

It's frightening war has started,

from peace we have departed.

It would be nice if politicians were pacifists,

oh that I wish.

It's hard to sometimes change people's point of view.

To think from a new angle, sometimes you should do.

What ever happened to, 'make love not war.'

Without love we are poor.

It's sad that people will always disagree with violence.

But you have to know your side of the fence.

What ever happened to, 'you don't hurt my mate, & I won't hurt yours.'

People that believe this, need a round of applause.

It breaks my heart when I watch the news,

with every life lost we all lose.

I'm glad that most people are peaceful,

& don't like acts that are cruel.

I wish the 1st World War was, 'the war to end all wars,'

& that the others since nobody saw.

I just wish people could be kinder,

& the world had much more laughter.

Mutant cat

-

There is a new mutant cat.

With new DNA & all that.

They can talk & understand us.

I spoke to one on the bus.

He raved on about chasing rats,

because after all they're still cats.

-

The palm reader

-

Hold out your hand,

& I'll read your fortune.

Don't ask how, you won't understand,

just know these predictions might happen soon.

I can also read tea leaves,

& a crystal ball too.

All I need is money & your fortune I can see.

The river poem, from observations of our postures

–

Rushing water, with an old man fishing.

Oh no he caught a boot.

Along comes a strange man, making funny noises.

Words to accompany the Jean Michel Jarre song, 'Oxygen'

at 1:20

Talk

We live on a beautiful planet.

We are lucky.

We need to take care of it....., & to love it.

Now we can breathe, in outer space.

With a back pack, & a shield on our face.

Now we can breathe, in a space ship.

In our space ship.....we can travel through space.

This blue atmosphere, & the water too,

enable's us to live.......love & enjoy with you.

Sing

Oxygen is blue, Oxygen is blue.

Oh Earth yes, ha ha how we really love you.

Yes we do, yes we do, really, oh really, oh really love you.

Oxygen is blue, Oxygen is blue.

Oh Earth yes, ha ha how we really love you.

Plants make it blue, take good care of you.

Plants make it blue we'll take good care of you.

That's what we'll do...... that's what we'll do.

Oh Earth, oh yes.....how we really love you.

Poem inspired by St George's Day

-

All the best legends, have a striking story.

Of the courage of hero's, belief & a good jackanory.

In a nutshell, protection of people, against a villain.

Great meaning & symbolism.

Now a story, told by a million.

-

-

Black history month poem

-

-

Without a doubt, there is racism about.

People that can otherwise be nice, can be racist too.

But when anybody reaches a certain level of intellect,

they realize that we are all the same.

Were all human being's that is correct.

We all have feelings, emotions, culture, a sense of style & beliefs.

Life is greater in every way, when we realize were all the same.

Most of us are trying our best, playing the game that is life.

Poem of interesting words that came into my head

-

-

Wowlastic, fantasticle, wonderful & fantansia.

Imaginative, creative, superb & superdooper.

Sculpture, poetry & writingly good.

Artistic & magical.

-

-

Free writing to atmospheric music

-

This is quirky music playing.

It also strangely sounds old, I'm really saying.

To this music, I feel like praying.

The more I listen, the more I pick out certain sounds.

Quite meditative, I could just lay on the ground.

What wonderful soundscapes, I feel I'm escaping into a dream.

Biscuit eating exercise

The fact, that I'm going to take ten minutes to eat two biscuits,

make's me chew more slowly.

Oh, how the chocolate tastes so lovely, it's melting on my fingertips.

I'm also enjoying my coffee, with just a few sips.

On to the next biscuit, this one's a shortcake,

a better biscuit I really couldn't make.

My translation of "Nearness of the beloved one" by Goethe

On the beach,

I gaze into the bright sky.

I feel I can touch you, when I reach.

I also feel I can see you,

riding like a white horse on the waves.

Moving in your graceful way.

But still I wish you were really here,

sitting next to me.

Your beautiful eyes I could then see.

Transport for London poster poem

-

Help the blind, & be careful of their guide dog.

So look, think & have compassionate etiquette please.

-

Poem to cheer Jan up after her stroke

-

-

We were so sad to hear you're unwell,

& you can't complete your paper,

because that would be swell.

But look on the bright side,

you're with your sister, & in wonderful Leeds.

That is wonderful indeed.

So get well soon,

of which we'll be over the moon.

Poem to cheer up Isley after being hit by a car

-

I was sad to hear of your knock,

but I am glad to hear you're alright.

It must have been a fright.

I bet with the driver you wanted a fight.

Your clothes all torn & tattered,

but your boyfriend is looking after you,

so you can have a good natter.

-

Story dice poem

-

-

The bird flew from the cage.

It whistled like a flute,

& flew to freedom, over the lighthouse.

With the liberator cheering, dressed in a suit.

Claude Monet book poem, about first page opened

-

-

I opened the Claude Monet book,

& a close up of a painting came into view,

I took a look.

It showed grainy brushstrokes, made with a hog hair brush.

I liked the effect, very much.

The colour's are beautifully vivid,

that are loved by nearly every critic.

I love the impressionists, they move my soul.

They cheer me up, when I'm full of woe.

I love them definitely so.

<u>The River Thames poem</u>

<u>Inspired by "Street music" by Arnold Adoff</u>

<u>From the book, "Love that dog" by Sharon Creech</u>

-

The River Thames, is the heart of London's Town.

Majestic it curves & bends, around the famous landmarks.

The picturesque countryside, is where it starts.

The Thames Estuary, is where it ends.

It definitely looks beautiful, through a camera lens.

A boat trip, I really recommend!

-

<u>A poem based on the words 'paper,' 'agnostic,' 'hobby,' &, 'hay.'</u>

-

All you need is paper & a pen for poetry.

& of course your imagination, that is key.

You can write about something complicated,

such as being agnostic, or simple as making tea.

Writing poetry can be a hobby,

it can be serious or in between you see.

30

It can be a way of making money.

Like making hay while the sun shines.

Elvis Presley the super hero

-

As a child Elvis was dirt poor.

He read comics & dreamed of being a super hero, & attended a black church.

He dreamed of being something great, something more.

He sang at school, the kids went into a frenzy.

Elvis asked, "what did I do?"

& was told, "I don't know, but you were great."

Then he cut a record, just for his mum's birthday,

& was set on a path, of international fame & fortune.

Like his comic superhero's, he wore capes & a crown.

His dreams come true, & what a sound.

J.K. Rowling's Harry Potter

-

Harry Potter was adopted by his aunt's family,

was mistreated & had no money.

On his twelve birthday, he found out he was a wizard.

He was going to Hogwarts School of Witchcraft & Wizardry.

But a villain named Voldemort, who killed his parents was trying to kill him.

He faced a battle, that he must win.

At school he made many good friends, & they all helped him.

He was gifted at magic, & especially flying.

This story, will tug on your heartstrings.

He defeats & kills Voldemort, to the world peace he brings.

My perfect day

A response to Lou Reed's song, "perfect day"

My perfect day.

Waking up at home with my family.

They are the first I'll see.

Going to my poetry group.

My perfect day.

Enjoying writing poetry.

Creative I'll be, with my friends around noon.

My perfect day,

taking it easy, may I say.

A poem about the cold

Most people don't like the cold.

DJ's complain on the radio.

Old people often moan & rant on so.

Weathermen say, 'it's not nice it's too cold.'

But I don't mind the cold weather.

As long as I'm not ill with a cold.

But rather feeling better,

& not stuck outside at the end of my tether.

Calm (a group exercise poem)

They look like their praying,

in deep thought.

Looking like stone philosopher's.

Two big cliffs against the sea.

Looking like The Tower of London.

Released from trouble & stress.

Charm

It's good to have charm, & to call yourself a prince.

Then you can be prince charming,

with etiquette, manners & eloquence.

Cast a magical spell of language,

just like a white witch.

A stomach bug

-

-

Summer is here,

weather is hot.

Temperature is high.

You drinka drinka drinka,

& suffer from a stomach bug.

Bugger it I'm buggered.

Not in that way you're thinking but

I've got a tummy upset.

& I can't stomach it,

bugs me, it really bugs me.

When I think of our dear teachers indisposition.

I feel sorry for her stomach virus.

Or whatever it is?

We hope she gets better quick.

& is not in any pain.

& comes back as right as rain.

To simply guide us in our poetry dealings.

Why do they call a stomach ache a stomach bug?

After all there's not a bug flying about.

The type of bug you get in an old rug.

After all a computer bug is named after a real bug.

I don't know what I have.

But I cannot get myself off the lav.

My diagnoses is a stomach bug.

Textiles poem for Grace's teacher

I really love textiles,

it makes me smile.

I love to make & create things,

using the sowing machine, to create some garments with some bling.

It's one of my favorite lessons in school,

I look forward to it because it's cool.

Its fun picking out my favorite fabrics, & showing Miss what I can do.

Miss Tewson is a lovely teacher, my knowledge in textiles has just grew.

Maybe one day I might be a fashion designer. If so I'll always remember you.

The Dorset Coast Express (a title picked from a newspaper)

A loved steam railway in Dorset.

No doubt is some people's life's work.

Repairing the tracks, breaking their backs,

but definitely an appreciated job.

As people go to relax.

Poem inspired by a photograph of a Paris-Roubaix cyclist

I was in a winning position,

then I skidded on a cobble.

I wobbled, then thud, I was in the mud.

No longer in the leading group.

My front wheel with a twist.

An opportunity of a win missed.

A cycling poem transcribed from another poem from the poetry group

-

It's finished on this muddy road.

My ruined bike, dreams of a win all finished.

Not victory, but instead I did not finish.

Well I'll drown my sorrows, down the local pub.

Well back to training, for next year's race.

-

Chilli Plant

-

Chilli plants are great.

Have beautiful orange flowers,

& grow tasty orange Chilli's.

Giving food a kick.

Chocolate

-

-

I'm really glad I like chocolate.

No let me say, I love chocolate!

It's a pity it's not good for your weight.

But what the heck, chocolate is great!

Complicated

-

-

Learning new skills can be complicated.

But with talent the complicated can become simple.

Everyone is good at different things.

So don't be put off by complication,

it may just become simple.

-

Councillor

-

Today I met Maria, she is a councillor.

Voted into Southwark Council.

Pledged to help the community,

with the Liberal Democrat Party.

Look for the yellow rosettes, there she'll be.

Egyptian art

-

-

The artwork in Egypt is preserved because it's dry.

The lovely colour's so bright & vivid.

So now you know why.

Free writing to Leo Abrahams

-

-

This music is futuristic, strange, reflective & melancholy.

When I listen, this is what I see.

I love the guitar sounds with all their effects.

Now there are voices beautiful sounding.

With whistling which makes me happy.

Then trumpets again joyful, & a little soulful.

Glad I listened to this music it's magnificent.

Now there are drums, jazzy sounding.

If I could play like this, for me it would be astounding.

How to be happy

-

-

How to be happy, this is what I recommend.

Look on the bright side of things.

Manage your affairs well.

Make the best of things.

Try to get up early.

Always carry some money.

& remember,

the secret of being happy is being happy.

-

Isabard Kindom Brunel

-

Isambard Kingdom Brunel was a Victorian in the industrial revolution.

He dug the first Thames tunnel as a solution.

You see a bridge was not good because of the tall ships.

Digging the tunnel was full of mishaps.

Diggers got ill & died, poor old chaps.

People lived & worked in the tunnel.

Queen Victoria visited the kafuffle.

It's now used by the tube on The East London Line.

People travel through without realizing Isambard said, "this tunnel is mine."

Jazz, hope & India

-

Memories of India fill me with hope.

Especially when listening to jazz,

because India is kinda Jazzy.

-

Lisa's conscious face book postings

-

-

Lisa's face book is so conscious, she says things like.

I'm going to eat my takeaway.

I have a cold, not feeling in a good way.

I'm watching Big Brother on TV right now.

That Katie Hopkins is a right cow.

Na night sweet dreams, I'm going to bed now.

Noises of cars, the door bell, a rubbish truck & trains from the art room

'Sound poetry' in Chase Lynne's class

-

Veroom deroommm, brooom.

Ding doonng.

Eieraaah braaack braaack.

Rahhh dak dok, da da darr, whooo, tra la tra la tra la.

-

Portsmouth Football Club

-

Portsmouth are in division two.

They are the hero's in blue.

With passionate fans in the beautiful game.

Chanting out "Pompeii," Portsmouth's name.

Rotherhithe Shed

-

Rotherhithe Shed is great for the community.

People drop by with brick-a-brack, & make things you see.

They can make a dolls house out of anything,

or just have a cup of tea.

It gets people out of the house, to learn new skills.

Rotherhithe Shed is brill.

Spring

-

-

In spring the days get longer, sunnier & warmer.

The trees get greener.

The bulb flowers peak through.

The birds migrate to pastures new,

& baby animals are born, & summer is soon.

-

Summer

-

-

In summer the days are longer,

often warmer & sunny.

The crops have grown, making farmers money.

The birds love to sing.

Its good the things summer brings.

The bright colour's of Summer

-

-

I love the beautiful colour's of summer,

the bright light bathing everything, making it warmer.

The bright yellows of sunflowers,

the green tree leaves, giving them powers.

The baby animals, playing amongst the multi-coloured flowers.

The colourful birds singing & flying.

The coloured ripe fruit multiplying.

The blue swimming pools in use.

People sipping on cold orange juice.

People in pub gardens drinking beer.

Oh what a wonderful time of year.

The dog Squeegley

-

There was a scruffy dog called Squeegley, being a dog his hearing was amazing.

Oh how he wished he was human, he really was far too smelly.

Sadly dyeing very young, of a problem with his belly.

Reincarnated as a human, remembering he was a dog, he realised he got his wish.

Still with amazing hearing, so he became an Xfactor judge.

With a problem of over excitement, before he took a walk.

But was over the moon, that he could actually talk.

The Duke

Everyone thinks she's the boss.

She wears the crown & reads the laws.

I have to stand a few steps behind.

That I always have to do as she says when she's cross.

But she's not always the boss.

You see marriage is all about give & take.

The reaction I'd like from my children's books

A sound poetry poem

Leowhoo, deiooh whee yeah!

Wowahhiee seehi he heway.

Leowavee ligh whoo hoo!

The sun

Ahh the beautiful sun,

bathing us in warmth & light.

It gives us life, & makes our days bright.

The Thames metaphor

-

The Thames is the life blood of London.

It pulsates & pumps the oxygen.

It transports & ferries people & goods.

Without it Londinium & London would not have stood.

-

The Tate Modern

-

-

The Tate Modern is a perfect example of a disused building,

used successfully for the people.

A fantastic design outside & in,

everyone that goes there is glad they've been.

Picasso, Matisse, Cezanne, Dali & Co.

Masters of the 20th Century.

Alongside contemporary greats,

Hurst, Emin, Gilbert & George to name four.

It's currently been extended to delight even more.

So I say, 'go.'

Think of the great works of art you can see,

& you can say you saw,

which, will only make you want to see more.

What I hate

-

I hate my mental health problems,

especially when I upset someone.

I hate sometimes having no confidence,

in front of every one.

I hate friends constantly looking at their phones,

across the screen their fingers run.

I hate magic eye pictures,

I can't see a single one.

I hate baked beans, forced to eat them at school,

hated every single one.

I hate shops putting the receipt in the carrier bag,

you can't take things back without one.

Wheeler dealer

-

-

I'm a wheeler dealer, struggle to make ends meet.

When I go to the theatre I have a cheap seat.

You'll find me in East Street,

selling all kinds of knocked off stuff.

I don't have much money, but making it I love.

I just wish I had more,

& wasn't so flipping poor.

Limesford Road future

‐

It's a rainy grey day, on the 1st of February of the year 3150.

It's Isley day, the day she time travelled too.

A crowd gather round 16 Limesford Road,

& look at the blue plaque on the wall.

A lady gives a speech about Aaron & Isley.

They talk about the predictions, what he got right & true.

The house was saved from demolition due to the Isley books.

It's now a gallery, where people take a look.

Ring Ring Ring Ring

‐

‐

Ring Ring Ring Ring.

Jason says, "hallo."

I think, 'great I remembered the number.'

Ring Ring Ring Ring.

I know from last time, I remembered the number.

Jason says, "hallo."

Ring Ring Ring Ring.

Isn't the phone amazing, all you have to do is ring,

to stay in contact, & isn't that a cool thing!

God let me introduce to you 'David'

\-

An angle say's to God, "let me introduce you to David Bowie."

David says, "hi."

The angle says, "he's a musician, singer, artist, designer,

actor, trendsetter & all round good guy."

David says, "oh & don't forget a lover."

So God commands, "you're in sir."

Cinema

\-

Ah cinema, I just love it.

I remember queuing for hours to get a seat.

Its fabulous entertainment, & a million dollar business.

The Lumiere Brothers got their wish.

They knew that great films, people didn't want to miss.

It's great because it's not expensive,

& special effects they know what to do with.

They can tell any story, no matter what it is.

Ah cinema, I just love it.

Titanic

-

"The ship it's sinking!"

"Oh my God!" I shout, "are their safety boats?"

The violins still sing.

"Only a few, they're being lowered on ropes."

"It's women & children first, we hit an iceberg."

The boat started to tip up.

Then we heard crying, people got word.

This is terrifying, screaming could be heard.

I realised I was going to die.

"I won't make America," I cried.

"But at least the women & children will have survived."

-

Pro leave the E.U.

-

The E.U. is undemocratic,

& yet they make our laws.

They let everyone into our country,

more & more they pour.

That is reason enough to Brexit.

The E.U. we don't need it.

Pro E.U.

-

There have been no European Wars since the E.U.

I'm sure I'll persuade you of my view.

The E.U. creates jobs, money and wealth.

People are better together,

working together is clever.

Together is better to tackle problems.

So let's have the E.U. for everyone.

Colours poem

-

Who is red?

Father Christmas is red.

Liverpool Football Club are too,

& the Welsh dragon also.

Yes that's true.

Where is Blue?

You find it in the sky,

& the sea abroad.

The paints Ultramarine, Colbalt & Prussion are blue.

Yes that's true.

What is yellow?

Yellow is a Primary Colour on the colour wheel.

The leader's jersey in The Tour de France is yellow.

Banana's & Canary birds are too.

Yes that's true.

When is green?

Green occurs when you mix blue with yellow.

It is the colour of leaves, moss & grass too.

I'm so glad I'm not colour blind,

& can experience colours & be moved.

CoolTan's Poetry Group Poem Based on the Spice Girls 'Wannabe Rap'

Come to CoolTan for poetry.

These are the people you might see.

Writing with wit is Mr Gary.

Imagination for Charles is easy.

Sasha tells stories that you'll believe.

Brian writes Latin analytically.

Then there's our teacher the fabulous Isley.

As for me, simple words that rhyme easily.

Come to poetry, ah you'll see.

We are friends and get along easily.

Enjoying poetry that is the key.

Acknowledgements

Front Cover Artwork

-

It was laid out and designed on Photoshop by Jeff Crownson.

Thank You

-

Aaron would like to thank all of his family & friends for their ongoing love, support, & advice. He would like to thank his Cooltan Arts Poetry Group that comprised of the poets Charles, Gary, Brian, Sasha and Howard. He would like to thank his poetry teachers, Ed Mayhew, Olivia Furber, Isley Lynne, Chase Lynne, Andrea Spitso and Karis Halsall. He would like to thank CoolTan Arts. Lastly, he would like to thank everyone, including those he forgot to mention here, who have helped him accomplish a dream of publishing a book! **THANK YOU TO YOU ALL!**